"Dror Wayne has created the marketing handbook for our time.

Wonderfully readable with great anecdotes from his own business successes, with other straightforward examples bringing his theories to life.

Dror is not regurgitating the information already out there, instead, "Business Doesn't Grow On Trees" is a road map with clear signposts and explanations for you to plan your marketing strategy in a practical way.

If you want to launch and grow your business, read this book!"

- Jon Sumroy, CEO Carfoldio Ltd., inventor of the mifold grab-and-go booster seat.

I0491065

ABOUT THE AUTHOR

I started out writing this in the third person… but that's not really my style. So Hi, I'm Dror. I'm going to be talking to you throughout this book, so here's a little about me first.

I co-founded my first business, MAGNIV, in 2016, incorporated it as MAGNIV Photomagnets Ltd in 2018 and worked to establish it as the leading provider of event photomagnets in the London wedding and luxury events space. I started out knowing nothing about anything I've written in this book and did it all with no investment.

In June 2020, with MAGNIV closed due to coronavirus, I co-founded The Kosher Mask Co Ltd – growing the business and selling it under two months later.

In July, I began recording Acumen, my digital talk show, all about leadership, business and marketing and moved from London, UK to Israel.

Oh and then I graduated from University. Now the real party starts.

BUSINESS DOESN'T GROW ON TREES

USING MARKETING TO ATTRACT NEW CUSTOMERS, DRIVE SALES AND GENERATE REVENUE

TABLE OF CONTENTS

INTRODUCTION   1

YOUR PRODUCTS & THE MARKET THEY'RE IN   6

BUYER PERSONAS   12

BRAND MESSAGING & POSITIONING   18

BRAND IDENTITY   22

NAMING   29

BRAND DESIGN   31

BRAND LANGUAGE   35

WEBSITES   39

TYPES OF MARKETING   55

EVENT MARKETING   64

WRITE A BOOK 67

HOST A DINNER PARTY 69

SEARCH ADVERTISING 72

START A PRIVATE MAIL LIST 79

CARE FOR YOUR CUSTOMERS 82

GO FOR ROUND 2 100

CREATE A CUSTOMER FORUM 109

ACTIVATE YOUR TEAM 112

MANAGE REVIEWS 118

GET REAL ON SOCIAL 123

QUICK NOTES 129

MENTIONS 132

TALK TO ME 134

ACUMEN – THE DIGITAL TALK SHOW 135

INTRODUCTION

The saying goes:

"Doing business without advertising is like winking at a girl in the dark. You know what you're doing, but nobody else does."

It was first said by Stuart Henderson Britt and now it's a cliché that has been repeated millions of times.

The fact is, it's true – though I'd make some changes.

It's not just advertising, it's marketing.

Advertising is not the only way to spread the word about your business. In fact, in 2020, there are often far better ways, particularly if you're not a global corporation with a billion-pound budget.

That's really what we're covering here – other ways to market that don't involve television commercials and billboards.

"Nobody else" is a bit of an exaggeration – but the point stands.

Your mate standing next to you in the club, who you've nudged to let him know that you're trying to catch the girl's (or guy's) attention. He knows what you're up to.

But correct me if I'm wrong, it's not him you want walking down the aisle towards you or you would already have told him. He's not your customer.

"You know what you're doing" – I disagree. Even you don't know what you're doing.

Because your end goal is not the winking, it's the aforementioned wedding. Or one-night-stand. Your choice, I'm not judging. Either way, if s/he can't see your wink, s/he can't react.

Even if s/he did notice, by chance, as a strobe lit you up, you wouldn't see the reaction to be able to make your next move.

So you wouldn't know what you're doing. Because flirting has to be a two-way street of communication. You think you know what you're doing, but really you're just being creepy, you creep.

Occasionally, you'll get lucky. Pun intended. Occasionally someone else might do the work for you – your friend sets you up or word eventually spreads around. But that's slow and unreliable. There's a lot of noise in nightclubs – it's hard to whisper to others.

What you want to happen (don't deny it) is the guy/girl to notice you dancing and fall for you already. You walk over, take her hand, start dancing and the rest is history.

"But Dror, that only happens in Hollywood".

No, it doesn't. This isn't a dating book, but the analogy is still working, so I'm going to stick with it a bit longer.

If you stop hovering near the bar alone, two-stepping, waiting for some magic moment and put yourself myself centre-stage, get noticed for your (imperfect) dance moves and actually talk to people, things on the dating scene may finally pick up.

All of this goes for business. You're a professional in your field or you have a solid product idea, just like I know you're a great guy or girl. You've decided to set up a business. Mazal Tov. But no one knows and no one really cares.

You can wink in the dark, hoping that (a) a strobe light will flash over you at the right moment, (b) a friend will do the work for your or (c) word will get around manually.

Or you can brush up your image. Understand what you have to offer and how it benefits your target audience. Turn that into a solid brand.

You can launch a good website – that's been carefully planned out, well-written, well-designed, well-programmed – and continue to optimise it over time.

You can start marketing to generate demand and leads. There are dozens of platforms available – video, social, email, content, search, print, events, network. You can pick the ones that are right for you and start working on them.

Business doesn't grow on trees – but you can go out and get it.

I've written this book to break down how all this works.

Chapter 1 is about defining your products and fitting them to the market – you may have already done this, you may need to refine them.

Chapter 2 talks about creating your Buyer Personas (also known as Ideal Customer Profiles and many other names).

Chapters 3, 4, 5, 6 and 7 are about your brand. We start with the Brand Messaging and Positioning, move to a conceptual approach to Brand Identity, touch on naming and finally create the "Brand Book", comprising Brand Design and Brand Language.

Chapter 8 is about your website, including my 5 step process to launching a website – strategy, copy, design, programming and management. That's the end of Section 1 – the core aspects of marketing.

Chapter 9 provides the theoretical introduction you need to proceed to the next chapters by speaking about different types of marketing and how they tie together – such as demand/ lead generation and brand/ product marketing. This is where I touch on terms like the marketing funnel.

Chapters 10-20 each break down a idea you can use in your marketing. I can't cover every single platform, every single approach and strategy, in this book. Think of the trees for that much paper. Here are a few ideas which startups and modern, techy companies are executing, that you can too. They should get your mind going and understanding the potential out there.

Chapter 21 is a collection of quick thoughts I wanted to include, but didn't go anywhere else.

Appendix 1 tells you a little bit about some of the businesses I've mentioned in this book – great companies that I've used and happily recommend.

Appendix 2 is where you'll find my contact details and information about working with me.

Appendix 3 tells you about Acumen, my digital talk show.

CHAPTER 01

Your Products & The Market They're In

TURN YOUR GOODS & SERVICES INTO PRODUCTS

If we're going to be successful in marketing your business, we need to stop thinking about the goods you stock and the services you can deliver and start thinking about the 1-3 products that we're trying to sell to your customers.

This is particularly important with service providers, who tend to have many skills they want to offer as services – it's far more difficult to market 10 different services than 3 different products.

Think of a photographer, for example. A multi-disciplinary photographer can apply their skills to weddings, events, products, families, schools, architecture, landscapes, photojournalism, paparazzi, corporate branding, real estate, fashion and more. But if we tried to market all of those, it would be difficult – if not impossible – to come up with coherent messaging and branding that works for them all.

For the weddings, maybe our photographer wants to emphasise how fun, relaxed and easy-going they are – not getting in the way, having a great time with Brides and Grooms, delivering natural photos. For the corporate branding photography, they might want to emphasise their technical skill, wide range of equipment and how much attention to detail they'll put in to perfecting each shot.

The messaging is completely different, the clients are completely different, so we'd want the brand to be completely different. We'd want the website to be completely different. We'd need to use different marketing channels and advertise on different platforms – splitting the resources available.

To market a business well, you need a small number of very clear products. I'd say try to narrow it to a maximum of three (with variations of course).

At MAGNIV, after trying out different things, we settled on one product – event photomagnets.

The product was simple – our photographer and technicians would attend your event, take photos and print them on-site as magnets.

We don't offer regular event photography without the printing. We don't offer printing on paper instead of magnets. We don't offer save-the-date magnets, magnetic invitations, magnet printing for photos you already have… we tried all of that over time but focussed down onto one product.

Within that product, there were variants in the price for location, length of event, time of day and number of guests. There were also upsells – photo props, custom printed photo props, white labelling…

But our product became clear and easily marketable. MAGNIV meant one thing – event photomagnets. People knew us, people understood us and we could promote ourselves.

You need to have a one-sentence answer to the question, "what do you do?" that leaves no confusion. I never used to and it was a problem. I'd say, "well…. I can do this, I also do a bit of this, on the side I do that and I sometimes do that".

I'm working with a designer at the moment who has a whole host of skills.

She can do brand design, web design, graphic design. She designs e-books and online courses for coaches. She makes promo videos and wedding videos. Our first session was spent listing, on paper, all the different services she could offer. She couldn't answer the "what do you do" question at all.

We created three products that she's going to be focussing on in the new direction of her business. Her answer is now, "I realign well-established entrepreneurs' brands, websites and online presences with their goals and clients".

Sure, there are follow-up questions, but it's pretty clear what she does. You're not going to ask her to illustrate your children's book or design your print brochure. You are going to ask her for brand design, a new website and design in the digital sphere.

DISRUPT OR CONFORM?

In the startup world, everyone is trying to disrupt the market. Don't get me wrong, there's a lot of money to be made if you're successful in revolutionising the world. Businesses like Uber, AirBnb, Facebook, PayPal, Google disrupt. Silicon Valley, Boston, Tel Aviv, London, Barcelona and other startup ecosystems are packed with more disrupters-to-be. There are hundreds – if not thousands – of companies trying to disrupt and the pressure to follow them is big.

But remember, there's also a lot of untapped potential in conforming to a market, bringing a good product to the table with a solid brand, strong messaging and good marketing. You don't need to discover a new bean to make a great coffee people will pay for.

Decide which route you're going down, because everything will hinge on that.

WHAT'S THE COMPETITION?

You've got to understand the space you occupy within the market. Where do you relate to them in terms of price? You could be more expensive, the same or cheaper – but you need to know what they're doing because you can be sure that the customers are comparing.

By understanding the competition, you can make sure to differentiate yourself. You can avoid duplicating their messaging and create a standout brand.

CHAPTER 01 – KEY TAKEAWAYS

- Narrow down your products. You can't do everything and you can't market yourself doing everything.

- Goods and Services alone are not products.

- You don't have to disrupt – you can conform and be successful – but decide now.

- Answer "what do you do" in one, clear sentence.

CHAPTER 02

BUYER PERSONAS

Also known as Ideal Customer Profiles.

You are not your customers. Selling based on what you like about your products is not going to work. We need to get inside the heads of your buyers so that everything else we do is relevant to them.

What are they looking for? How are they looking for it? How do they make their decisions? What are they flexible about?

Imagine you sell a range of laptops:

- You've got regular laptops that suit students with a limited budget, able to handle Word, Powerpoint, Excel, Chrome and Outlook. (Product 1)

- You've got lightweight, sleek laptops that handle the same basic functions, but load very fast and cost significantly more, for CEOs and travelling executives. (Product 2)

- You've got high-performance laptops that suit gamers, designers, coders and video editors, with extra RAM, huge hard drives and massive processing power. (Product 3)

The students care about budget and size. They want to know they're getting the best deal on a laptop that will see them through university, getting their work done and maybe watching Netflix in bed.

For the executives, money isn't so important. They want to know they're getting an exclusive product. They want it to be fast, slim and good looking.

For the creatives and gamers, the tech is everything. They want to know the exact specs and will compare the details.

So for each product, you'll write different ads, different landing pages and different sales emails. The 50 year-old lawyer isn't going to understand what you mean by i9 quad-core processor, 256GB SSD and true-colour screen technology. They're also not likely to be looking on Instagram for their new laptop.

Your Buyer Personas are to help us get into your customers' heads. Do they want to have a salesperson WhatsApp them or email them? Will they react better to being addressed as Mr/Mrs/Miss/Ms/Dr or by their first name? Do they watch

YouTube "influencers" unboxing products or read reviews on the website?

Having established the purpose of Buyer Personas, let's talk about how to create them.

I think this is one of those things best done as a team, with a whiteboard, various coloured markers and of course, refreshments. Gather 3-5 people in a meeting room and start with your first persona. Everyone gets to call out details about this person and it all goes on the board. Once the board is full, take a photo of it, wipe the board and move on to the next persona. Afterwards, type all the notes up and hand them over to your designer – ask them to create a visual profile which will become part of your company's internal marketing documentation.

Your Buyer Personas should be:

- Visual

- Specific

- Wide-ranging

- Realistic

Visual

You should be able to close your eyes and picture each of your BPs. That's why we give them names and physical characteristics. If they're in an office, what does it look like? If they're in a bedroom, is it clean or messy?

If we're talking about a senior executive with decision making power, that could be anyone.

If you're talking about Gerald, the 55 year-old, 165cm man, who maintains a good shape by going to the gym 3 times a week and walking to work in his pinstripe suit... now I have a visual picture of the person I'm trying to sell to.

Specific

Your BP should be so specific that it's slightly less accurate.

Melissa, the 32 year-old working Mum to whom you're marketing a holiday resort, might not actually like denim jackets, even though that's what your BP said.

You might say she uses an iPhone and drives an SUV, when in fact she uses a Samsung and drives a Prius. But the more specific picture helps us work.

That's why we say Melissa uses an iPhone with a cracked screen because her 6-year old threw it on the floor when Peppa Pig stopped playing because the internet was too slow.

The real, specific, human picture we paint helps us understand the trends and pains that face the customer.

Wide-ranging

The more topics you cover in building a BP, the better. I've mentioned technology, dress, habits, fitness and family. What about interests, foods and politics? What do they do in their free time? Are they more Netflix or Audible? It all helps.

Realistic

There's no point building a BP that is too whacky and becomes inaccurate. If your BP seems strange or unusual, it's probably not representative.

You should be able to look back at your BP and think "this is exactly like someone I know". In fact, you should be able to look back at your BP and think that's like a lot of people you know – your previous and existing customers.

Have you heard of Karen? That's a persona! Though unfortunate to the many people actually named Karen out there (I know some who are really nice), when people talk about Karen, everyone instantly pictures the same woman, in her 40s, with the same hairstyle, asking to speak to the manager.

By putting a few hours into creating good Buyer Personas now, you're investing in a resource you'll be able to come back to over and over again in the future.

CHAPTER 02 – KEY TAKEAWAYS

- You are the best person to build your Buyer Personas.

- Don't just think of your current customers but of your ideal customers.

- Make your BPs Visual, Wide-ranging, Specific and Realistic so they're valuable.

CHAPTER 03

BRAND MESSAGING & POSITIONING

We've broken down your products. We understand where you sit in the market, individually and relative to your competitors. We also understand your customers – what they're looking for, what their pain points are.

Now we can develop the messaging and positioning we want your brand to portray.

This can be somewhat reworded later on if need be, once we've worked on the Brand Language.

Start by listing the key sales/marketing messages – features and benefits that you offer with each product. Why should someone choose you?

Some people like to write out a mission, vision and values. For the sake of marketing, I like to write a promise, positioning statement, three pillars and founders' message.

For our laptop store, the promise could be, "the right laptop for every person". It's what you as a business deliver, simply put.

The positioning statement is longer, explaining what you do. It's not, "TetraLaptops sells laptops and accessories", rather "TetraLaptop matches people and businesses with the best work laptop for their needs, together with all the accessories to get the job done".

Your pillars are three nouns or adjectives, which should sum up the way your business operates and the sales messages. I write each pillar in a table, with a sentence explaining what it means and 2-3 practical examples. Here's an example from one client:

Pillars

Reliability	Systematic Transparency	Technology
Just consider it done, like clockwork. Don't think, let alone worry, about the details.	We're fully accountable to you, by virtue of the system.	Our full investment means your best results.
• Vetted, in-house staff • All staff in uniform • All our own products and equipment • Reporting to control centre	• View staff information • GPS-verified clock-in/out • Before & After photos All accessible, immediately, for every job, 24/7 via the platform.	• Electric vans and other environmentally-friendly measures • Our custom-built digital platforms • The latest techniques, machinery and products

I then write a page about each pillar in more detail, followed by the Founders' Message, which is a more personal touch – Founders tend to embody the Brand's Messaging and Positioning themselves.

By now, we should have:

- A Promise

- A Positioning Statement

- Three Pillars, explained

- A Founders' Message

- A list of Key Sales & Marketing Messages

- Buyer Personas

So as we move into the next stages, we have lots of concrete foundations to go on. Our designers will understand what they're trying to portray when they design a logo and our copywriters will be able to craft more tailored websites and emails.

CHAPTER 03 – KEY TAKEAWAYS

- It's time to put the foundations of your brand on paper.

- Don't worry too much about the wording – this is for internal use more than external.

- This is all to guide your marketing and sales moving forward. Don't cut corners – everything is based on this.

CHAPTER 04

BRAND IDENTITY

If your business were a person, how would people describe it?

Kind, caring and generous?

Daring, adventurous and energetic?

Wise, patient and studious?

The last holistic stage of brand development is looking at the messaging and positioning you've written down, looking at the Buyer Personas you're trying to appeal to, looking at your products and their benefits to customers and creating the brand identity or brand character.

And that all comes down to one simple question – if your business were a person, how would people describe it?

Or better yet, how do you want people to describe it?

Don't try and build a sexy business if your products are and customers want discreet corporate.

Don't assume you have to be "professional", which really means stuffy, boring and robotic, if your product is a fun and fresh addition to the market and your customers are open-minded, energetic people.

Many people use the 12 Brand Archetypes to help understand their brand identities. I've used them with some customers successfully but at other times I've found they don't quite work. I'll introduce them here though if you'd like to use them in developing your brand I'd advise you do some online research.

These were developed by the Swiss psychologist Carl Jung in the early 20th century.

I won't delve too deeply into what he believed and how he came up with these, but what's important to understand is that the 12 Brand Archetypes are different "characters" which cover the full spectrum of personalities.

In analysing different brands, you'll easily be able to associate some with one of the archetypes.

The archetypes aren't set in stone, however. Most businesses need to create their own blend of 2, 3 or even 4 archetypes.

What's more, different people understand the archetypes differently. It's fascinating to work with a wide variety of clients, brand strategists and designers, seeing their own interpretations and applications of the archetypes.

Some people even divide each archetype into 3-5 sub-archetypes!

So if you're reading about them online, make sure to use a few different resources, created by different people, to give you a more broad perspective.

The 12 Brand Archetypes are:

The Hero

This one is pretty easy to understand. The Hero rides over the hill to save the day. A natural leader. Inspiring, motivating. You're inclined to follow. Strong, skilled, good-looking.

The Ruler / Royal

The Ruler is the ultimate luxury and will never settle for anything less than the best. Tailored suits, designer dresses. Leather seats, chauffer-driven cars. Power. Prestige. Perfection.

The Rebel / Maverick / Outlaw

The Rebel is everything the Ruler isn't. Screw the rules. Forget the norm. The Rebel is down and dirty. The Rebel doesn't drive a Mercedes, they drive a Harley. The Rebel wears leather jackets and has studs and tattoos. Authentic in a point-to-prove, contrary kind of way.

The Entertainer/Jester

The Entertainer is the life of the party. Upbeat, friendly, extroverted. They're bright and colourful, full of joy and very engaging. They'll hold anyone and everyone in conversation.

The Sage

The Sage is wise and is all about learning. They believe in knowledge, research and development. They use statistics, facts and information. They share their knowledge with others and want to gain more. That's how they better the world.

The Explorer

The Explorer wants to get off the beaten path. Authentic in a curious way. Doesn't require luxury, doesn't require attention – just wants to get going and see what's over that hill, what's inside that cave or at the top of that mountain.

The Everyman/ Woman (The Guy/ Girl Next Door)

The Everyman is supposed to be your "average" person, whatever that means. If you walked past them every day but then were asked to describe them, you'd struggle, because they're so... forgettable. Genuine person, in casual clothes, nothing to stand out.

The Creator

The Creator might not be the loud centre stage, but they view the world as a canvas. They're full of colour, art and expression – whether it's music, performance, building or coding. The Creator doesn't believe in restrictions.

The Lover

The Lover is sensual, passionate and luring. Their exquisite style draws you towards them – they're soft, sexy and daring. With a a sparkle in their eye, you know there's something more they're implying but it doesn't need to be said out loud.

The Magician

The Magician wows you with the experience they create – you just don't know how they do it. You don't see the hard work – only the final product.

The Innocent

The Innocent is carefree, fun and good. They want to just enjoy life in a safe, simple way. They view the world as a great place to be and keep things pure.

The Caregiver

The Caregiver is the generous archetype. They look out for others in a selfless, altruistic way. Their entire raison d'etre is compassion, nurturing and helping others. They're stable, quiet and reliable.

It's up to you to decide if these are helpful for you in formulating your brand identity. For many, they're a useful tool in actualising a vision. But don't allow them to limit you.

Whilst developing your brand, you can pick out other brands and try to explain what it is about them that you identify with – and equally as important, what it is about them that you don't identify with.

You can also draw on celebrities, characters in culture and famous people... Are you more James Bond, Meghan Markle or Alan Sugar? Why?

CHAPTER 04 – KEY TAKEAWAYS

- Personify your business – it makes it far easier to understand.

- The business identity isn't necessarily the same as your personal identity (unless you're a one-person service business). Think about the products and the buyers.

- The 12 Brand Archetypes are a useful tool for approaching brand identity, but don't get held back if they don't work for you.

- This is all about being descriptive and visual. It's for you, not your customers.

CHAPTER 05

NAMING

If you haven't already named the business, this is the time to do it, because we've done the groundwork on the brand, but we can't continue to Brand Design without the name.

The important things to check with a name are:

- Trademarks, copyright and other businesses (you don't want to get into trouble and be forced to change)

- Pronunciation – can everyone pronounce it? Will people pronounce it correctly when they read it?

- Spelling – when people hear it, will they be able to write it down correctly? This is important, because they need to be able to type the name into Google and find you.

- Alternative meanings and foreign languages – check the dictionary, check the urban dictionary, do a google search for "name + meaning" and ask some friends. You can't check every dialect on the planet, but you can do an hour's research to be sure.

The name of a company really isn't that important – you've got to tick the basic boxes, but after that, it's more about what we do with the name that the name itself.

Imagine if Apple was called Uber, Uber was called Google and Google was called Hilton. Crazy to think, but I'm sure they'd be as successful today.

It's the same as naming a baby. It's rare, but it may be changed at a later date. Chances are, they'll grow into the name, make it their own and it will stick, as long as you don't choose something stupid. Just pick a name already, so that the kid can get on with its life.

CHAPTER 06

BRAND DESIGN

Design really isn't my area, so this is going to be pretty short.

At this stage, you should be hiring a brand design specialist and providing them with all our foundational work. They will create proposals for you to look over, choose your favourite from and request revisions. Once you get it down, they'll turn it into a BrandBook and send you over the files and your initial applications.

Brand Design includes:

- Typography (the business's fonts)

- Colours (the business's core palette)

- Shapes, styles and icons

- A Logo

That's pretty much it. You then want your initial applications, based on that:

- Letterhead (and digital letterhead)

- Business Cards

- Uniforms (if necessary)

- Merchandise (if budget allows)

Uniforms are for jobs where the staff will need to wear them. Security guards, cleaners, caretakers, gym instructors, event technicians wear uniforms to be clearly identifiable. If you want to get branded clothing that isn't needed for staff, that comes into merchandising.

The reason I say you should get some merchandise now is not really for marketing purposes – in fact, in terms of marketing, merchandise isn't the greatest investment early on. Better to spend that money on digital in most cases. But it is good for building the authority of the brand and loyalty to it.

You want to see your brand identity around so it fills you with pride and more importantly – you want your team to be proud of the business they're working in. Giving them each a tshirt, notepad, pen, some stickers, a mask, a lapel pin... it builds up that emotional attachment. Don't blow too much money, but if you've got the budget and will want merch, there's no harm in buying it at this stage.

Plus, we're going to need a photoshoot soon – before we dive into the website – so you may as well have your uniforms and merchandise to include in the pictures.

When you're hiring a designer and evaluating portfolios, look at the explanations behind their work. They'll often show examples and explain what the brief was and how they expressed that in the design.

Design isn't (just) about making things pretty. It's as much a science as an art.

It's also not about you liking it. What you like might not be the best thing for your business. So deal with it and trust the designer.

CHAPTER 06 – KEY TAKEAWAYS

- Design is not about looking pretty.

- Design is not about what you like.

- By giving the designer all the materials we've already created, they'll be able to create a brand design that reflects it accurately and meets our goals – and that's what matters.

- Your designer will pick fonts, colours and styles now. Once they're finalised, stick with them. Consistency is key.

- Merchandise isn't great for marketing, but it's nice to have. If the budget is there, go for it, why not. Make sure it's on brand. Cheap throwaway pens are not on brand for a big corporation.

CHAPTER 07

BRAND LANGUAGE

Here's to all the writers out there, so often overlooked.

Hey people, your BrandBook should include language also. This part is often called a Tone of Voice Guide, Editorial Style Guide or Language Style Guide.

Your brand language needs to suit your audience, suit you and be consistent. That's not easy, especially when a lot of people are writing on behalf of your company – emails, notifications, press releases, blogs, ad copy…

Including Brand Language in your BrandBook is important for keeping everyone on the team – no matter how big or small – consistent.

I'll give you a run-down on some things you can include in your brand language, but you can also find lots of real-life examples from big brands online (yeah, people publish their style manuals on their websites).

Write lists of nouns, adjectives, verbs and adverbs that reflect your company. You don't want everyone to just use the words "good", "nice" and "big". Do you want them to use "Pretty", "Beautiful", "Breath-taking", "Presentable", "Elegant", "Handsome" or "Stunning"? These imply slightly different meanings... but aren't that different. If you're renting out an apartment, which one employee describes as "pretty" and another describes as "handsome", there's something not adding up.

Describe the tone and style you want writers to adopt. Is grammar a priority or is the priority being easy to understand? Are you fussed about dangled prepositions, split infinitives and the passive voice?

Do you use American or British spelling? What about the Oxford Comma?

Active or Passive Voice?

Should your writing be formal or informal? Do you use emojis, slang and acronyms? Do you use technical jargon or simplify your language? Should sentences and paragraphs be long or short?

Include plenty of examples, so your writers know what you're trying to get them to do.

Does your company prefer writers to use the single or plural? (I or We?)

Do you want to use the imperative? (Sign up now). Perhaps you prefer to inform (You can learn more here).

Create a jargon-buster, if it's important that your people avoid jargon. Sometimes, we don't even notice we're using industry language instead of customer language. Help your people translate their language into customer language.

Remember to include any specific formatting notes for brand terms. MAGNIV is always spelled in capitals, for example. That's a brand decision we made and now needs to be stuck to. Write a list of what should be capitalised, hyphenated, etc.

Brand Design + Brand Language = BrandBook

Ask your designer to create a BrandBook for you, including all the information you've collated from these two chapters into one, clean document. Every employee should have a copy saved to their desktop and it should be part of new employee onboarding. Y'know what, if you've got the budget, get it printed and have a few copies lying around the office.

CHAPTER 07 – KEY TAKEAWAYS

- A consistent writing style is important.

- If your vocabulary is limited to "big", "nice" and "good"… there's a problem.

- Language matters – there's a lot of thought that goes into it.

- Consider a Jargon-Buster – the language you use should reflect your customers.

CHAPTER 08

WEBSITES

Many people are under the (false) impression that to get a website, you need to hire a web designer. Design is important, but there are actually five stages to creating your website:

- Strategy & Planning

- Copy

- Design

- Programming

- Launch & Optimise

In fact, with all the brand groundwork we've done, once we've created the web strategy, the design should be fairly simple (unless you're spending extortionate amounts on extraordinary web design).

If you follow these five stages in order, your website will do the job it's meant to. It's that simple. If, instead, you just hire a web designer on Fiverr… you're wasting your time and money.

The thing is, every business needs a website. I can't think of a single business that would not benefit from a website.

Even if your has managed so far without a website, you'll be able to grow once you've launched a website with these five stages. If you've previously had a website that hasn't worked, so you think you're better off with out one, you just had a rubbish website. Sorry not sorry.

Plus, these days, websites are so cheap, there's no excuse for not launching one. If you're bootstrapping and can't afford a copywriter, designer and programmer, just use Squarespace. If you've done the ground work on your brand already and you think carefully about the Strategy and Copy (we'll get to that), it will do the job just as well.

Why Squarespace? Wordpress and Webflow are a step up. They're for pro designers and programmers. If you're an experienced designer and really want to step it up, put days into your website and make it completely custom, go for Webflow. Spend a day watching all their tutorial videos and you'll be set.

Otherwise, use Squarespace because their websites are fully responsive. Unlike certain other drag-and-drop design platforms which shall remain nameless, you don't actually have full control over Squarespace and that's a good thing.

You drag blocks and objects to sit in relation to one another – not to a specific point on the page – so if someone is viewing your website on a laptop, tablet or mobile with a different sized screen to yours, Squarespace can adjust automatically. No need for side-to-side scrolling.

Want a secret? My own website is on Squarespace and we also built The Kosher Mask Co's website on Squarespace. I did it pretty much in one night. You pick a template, input your brand colours and the rest of the design work is pretty much done for you. Even terrible designers like me can manage.

Whether you're bringing in a pro or doing it yourself, I'll now take you through the five stages in more detail.

Strategy

Don't fall into the trap of thinking, "I'll put a Home, About, Blog and Contact page and my website is done". That works for some businesses, but it's become too common for no good reason. Instead, start by answering the following questions:

What do I want my customers to do?

Do you want your customers to make an online purchase from your e-commerce store? Do you want them to make a reservation online? Contact you via a form? Or if your business is fully brick-and-mortar and you just want them to turn up, are you simply aiming to persuade them to come?

The entire customer journey on the website should be guiding them towards these goals. Don't just think about what "looks cool". Think about how you're going to bring the customer to the finish line, in a way that represents your brand.

What do my customers want?

At the same time, we can't just focus on what we want. We have to focus on them. What are your customers looking for? What information might they be seeking?

At the end of the day, you do want to meet customer demands in order to achieve your goals. Giving customers the right information improves their buying experience – whether it's directions to your location, care instructions for your product or the answers to FAQs.

Make a list of all the things you want your customers to do and all the things your customers want. Sort them by order of importance.

We can use that list to start planning the pages and the content on each. Let's compare and contrast a restaurant and a law firm.

Customers like to view the menu before visiting an eat-in restaurant. They want to see what's on offer, what the prices are and maybe look at photographs of the various dishes. That way they can decide if the restaurant is for them.

You might want to focus on putting an Online Booking Form to collect reservations first – but that won't meet the customer needs if they can't find the menu. If a customer can't find a menu on your website and instead has to rely on an out-of-date, blurry photograph of a partial menu someone has uploaded to TripAdvisor, they're more likely to just go elsewhere – even if your reservation form is front and centre.

You've got to prioritise the menu or at least put the buttons for both next to each other... but to push your conversions, consider putting a button at the bottom of the menu leading to the reservation form.

For a law-firm billing cases hourly, most people aren't expecting fixed prices. They're not expecting a menu.

They're expecting to be able to go to an expert in the field of law they need, who can provide everything in that sector.

They also don't need to see pictures of the décor and ambience in the office – it's not as relevant as it is in a restaurant.

The price tag also tends to be much higher, so whilst people may be willing to "just try out" a new restaurant, they're going to put more care into selecting a law firm.

What they do need to see is that you're experts and trustworthy. So you may prioritise social proof – listing well-known brands who use your firm and sharing case studies of previous wins. You may also highlight each staff member and their career history – it's important to know who you're choosing as a lawyer. No one really cares how many years the waiter has been serving pizza, as long as the Chef knows what s/he's doing.

So grab a pen and paper – or whiteboard markers, if you're in a team – and start mapping out your pages. Just sketch to get an idea of what you're thinking in terms of buttons, headlines, subtitles and paragraphs.

This is known in the design world as a wireframe.

If there are any particular images you want in certain places, include those, but you can generally leave that stuff to the designer. Your pages should look something like this:

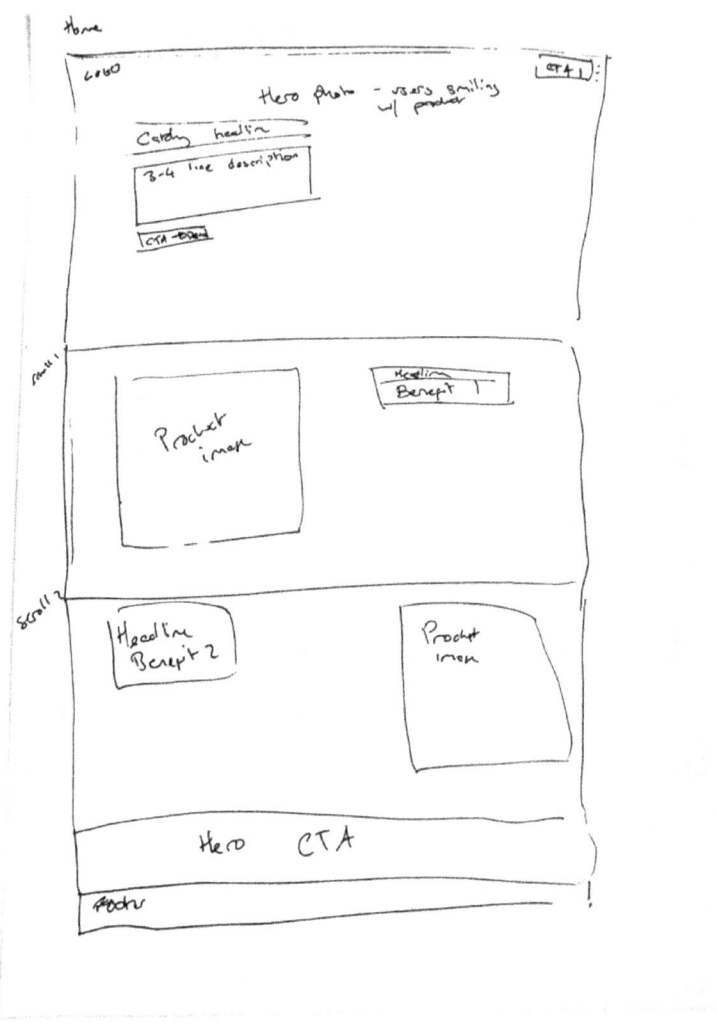

I know, that's messy and basic. But that's your wireframe (just personalise it to your company).

Remember, there's an important balance to be struck when planning website content.

On the one hand, you want it to be different – stand out – from all the other websites out there. You want a total user-focus that guides visitors to the conversion pages and represents your brand fully.

On the other hand, you need to stick with what people know. Don't hide things in obscure places or make people click around in circles to get to important information.

Similarly, remember that simple is often best. Do you really need Google Maps embedded on your contact page? If most people are viewing your website on mobile, that map is going to be annoying – better just put a link on the address and their phones will automatically open the map in app.

One important factor in the user experience (UX) of a website – and by extension, SEO, as Google is focussed on giving the best UX – is loading speed.

The more junk you fill up your website with, the slower it will load. So choose wisely. How many blocks do you really want to embed? Does that autoplay video really add anything? Is a chatbot right for you? We'll talk later about the tech stack, but when planning pages, don't add features for the sake of it.

Think of the user with the bad internet connection, no patience and lots of money to spend. You don't want them leaving your website to go to a competitor because your animated homepage isn't opening yet.

Copy

Once that's done, it's time to get writing. Have the BrandBook next to you – it will make life a lot easier – and just start putting words down on paper. Write as you talk and keep it short. You'll be able to come back and edit later.

Make sure you've used spellcheck on word and run the text through Grammarly, just to be safe!

Remember what I said about the balance between standing out and sticking with what people know? That applies to copy also. If you're explaining where your business is located, use something like "how to find us", "where we are", "getting here". Not, "What's your 20?" because although you might think you're cool, you're just making life harder. Remember, my grandmother could be on your website, planning my birthday surprise. Don't make it harder for her.

I love words. With long, complex sentences you can create such a vivid picture in the reader's mind. The power of penmanship rivals the most deadly weapons.

But...

Your website copy needs to be short.

People don't read long paragraphs.

Make.

It.

Shorter.

Get it? Good. Moving on.

Design

Did I mention I'm not a designer? I did, didn't I?

Luckily, this is pretty simple:

Make sure you stick with your brand design and your web strategy and the rest should just fall into place.

Of course, if you've got a good designer, they'll be able to bring it a level up.

Whichever you choose, remember the "be unique" vs "play by the rules" balance. It applies in design too. For example, everyone knows that three dots/lines means menu (aka the burger). They click it, various buttons appear. Don't go hiding your menu behind a triangle and assume that people will know what it does.

Programming

These days, websites don't need programming like they used to. Many platforms such as WebFlow cut out the need for coding everything and you can achieve some pretty powerful stuff without typing out a line of code.

But there is still some programming to do, such as installing your tech stack.

Marketing in 2020, it's important not to get too caught up in all the tools and tech – our audiences are becoming desensitised to automation. It's true that good creative (which AI is yet to replace) is where you can shine.

Nonetheless, get the tech on your website sorted. Make sure you've got all the Googles set up – Google Analytics, Google Ads, Google Search Console and Google My Business at least. You may also want to look into Google Optimise and Google Tag Manager.

There are other useful tools – but remember that the more you install, the slower your website will be. So only install those that you're actually planning to use.

- Drift is great for Live Chat and Chatbots – or as they call it, conversational marketing.

- HotJar is useful if you're at the stage of analysing user behaviour. You can watch screen recordings of individual sessions to understand where you're losing customers and create exit pop-ups to collect feedback.

- Unbounce is useful for varying landing pages with ad campaigns.

- Privy is solid for all things e-commerce

- Typeform is the way to go for great-looking forms embedded in your site.

Programming is also important when it comes to SEO. You need to make sure the right pages have the right tags, so Google knows what to index. If you've got duplicate content, make sure to implement a redirect. Put good metadata on all your pages (without exception) and structure your copy with the right header tags. Make sure your photos are compressed to a reasonable file size and all include alt text. For most basic business websites, it shouldn't get much more complex than that.

Quick trick for getting your website indexed fast… copy and paste every URL into Google Search Console. Now, the techy SEO experts will tell you this isn't necessary and if your sitemap is done properly, Google will index it automatically. They're probably right, but in my experience, it speeds things up. Similarly, every time I publish a new blog or update a page, I copy and paste the URL into GSC for indexing.

Launch & Optimise

The next stage is so important...

Don't laugh...

You have to actually launch your website.

Crazy, right?

But I see so many people who run into roadblocks in getting their website perfect... so they don't launch it at all.

But here's the thing.

The beauty of YOUR website is that YOU are in control.

You can always take it down again. You can always change that title, edit that spelling mistake (which shouldn't have been made, but life happens) and you can always tweak the colours.

For now though, GET IT UP. Because each day without the website is harming your business.

So you've got a photoshoot scheduled for after your uniforms arrive in two weeks and want to include real pictures on the site. I get it and I totally agree. But if everything else is ready, launch the site TODAY using stock photos and come back later to adjust.

Once you've launched, keep optimising it. Look at your analytics data at least every fortnight and see where the problems are.

If people are going to your FAQ page and then disappearing, maybe you need to change an FAQ which is causing the problem – or maybe you just need to add a CTA (call-to-action) on a button after the questions.

Which is your slowest loading page? Why? Can you fix it?

Is there a page performing particularly well? Can you work out why? Can you replicate that feature? Can you promote that page more?

Make sure your content is up-to-date and fresh. If you're changing your opening hours for the holidays, closing for refurbishment, on furlough due to a global pandemic... update your website (along with your GMB and Facebook Page) as soon as possible.

The only thing more annoying than your favourite restaurant being closed... is your favourite restaurant being closed when their website, Google Maps and Facebook Page all say they're open, so you get dressed and meet friends there but can't go in.

Am I right?

So don't be like that.

Make updating your website a priority.

And because you're going to need to update your website regularly, now you should make sure you've got a simple Content Management System (CMS). If you have in-house programmers, fine, it can all be buried in the code. Otherwise, whether your website is custom-built from scratch or based on a template, you need to be able to access the CMS and make your own changes. That's another reason I'm a fan of Squarespace and Webflow.

CHAPTER 08 – KEY TAKEAWAYS

- Websites are more than just design.

- Start by planning the content based on what your audience want and what you want.

- Remember to keep updating and improving your site.

- It's important to get the website up, rather than pushing it off for ages

That's the end of the first section. You've now got the fundamentals which apply to all businesses. Moving forward, here are ideas from you to choose from and taking inspiration from.

CHAPTER 09

TYPES OF MARKETING

I don't want to get too technical here – this book is meant to be very practical.

However, understanding some of the key technical concepts is important so that you understand where your different campaigns and channels fit into the big picture of your marketing.

The Marketing Funnel

All our efforts to find and acquire customers – in both sales and marketing – can be placed in the big picture we call "The Funnel".

Picture a funnel – wide at the top, narrow at the bottom. At the top, our marketing efforts are targeting many people. The objective is to convince as many of the right people to continue to travel through the funnel until they drop out the bottom – and buy.

So different marketing campaigns may be described as "top of the funnel", "middle of the funnel" or "bottom of the funnel". Colloquially in the marketing world, you might hear these referred to as TOFU, MOFU and BOFU. We're not talking about vegetarian food alternatives ☺

The top of the funnel is where we build awareness of a brand and its products. You might not be able to track direct, financial ROI from your TOFU marketing. Many broadcast advertising forms – such as newspaper ads, billboards and television ads – are top of the funnel.

You may also launch targeted social media ads based on demographics and interests as part of your TOFU marketing. A sportswear brand may launch ads on Facebook and Instagram to target young people interested in sports, gyms and exercise. There's no guaranteeing that those people will be at all interested, but we're just getting the ideas in front of them to start off with.

"Sales Development Representatives" making cold-calls and door-to-door salespeople are also targeting the Top of the Funnel – they're just doing it one at a time, whilst in the marketing world we work en-masse.

Middle of the funnel is building on our awareness work at TOFU to establish interest. This is where we get more specific in the benefits of products. You've got people in already, now it's time to start displaying the product and talking about the benefits it provides. Your content here is more targeted and you may choose to engage tactics such as remarketing – using cookies to send ads to people who have previously visited your site or clicked on your ads.

BOFU is where you trigger your interested prospects to consider purchasing. Here, you're going to be helping them make the right decision. Personal product demos and proposals tailored to a customer's needs are essential in the bottom of the funnel. Pop-ups offering discounts to customers who are about to leave a website; abandoned-cart emails automated through software such as Privy; turning up at the customer's office with a contract, pen and credit card machine is making the final push through the bottom of the funnel.

So when considering different marketing campaigns, bear in mind where in the funnel they fall. Is it a brand awareness campaign, at the top of the funnel? Or is it a conversion campaign at the bottom of the funnel?

If it's TOFU, you can't evaluate it based on purchases. So choose metrics or Key Performance Indicators that reflect awareness – such as impressions – and think about how you're going to start turning the awareness into interest.

If it's BOFU, then you want to be measuring sales – hard revenue. Think about how your copy and creative are encouraging purchases – because these people are already aware, they've shown interest and now your job is to convert.

As we go through the next 10 chapters, think about how each idea can fit in the funnel. But first, let's take a look at the different "jobs" that marketing fulfils.

Demand Gen

Demand Generation is about getting people interested in the product you have to offer. Rather than turning up at their front-door and begging them to buy, you're emphasising the problem you solve or building a vision of the luxury you offer. Demand Gen is generally at the TOFU level and includes both inbound and outbound marketing techniques.

Lead Gen

Like Demand Gen, Lead Gen does exactly what is says on the tin. Its aim is to acquire the data of prospective customers, with whom your team can follow up and close a deal. Gated content (giving access to content, such as an e-book or article, only once someone gives their email address) is a good example of Lead Gen.

It may be the sales team that follows up with the leads you generate or they may go into a marketing sequence – drip email campaigns, retargeted ads, automated special offers...

Sometimes it can be confusing – are you doing Demand Gen or Lead Gen? Don't worry too much about it, because often they're very similar. It may also just depend on your offering.

If what you offer is a product that people go on Amazon to buy, you may focus on Demand Gen with the aim that people will eventually go to buy it from Amazon.

If you have a more expensive product or a B2B product and tend to engage customers in sales calls once they've expressed interest, you might want to put more emphasis on Lead Gen.

Sales Enablement

Sales Enablement is where marketing serves the sales team. We as marketers want to give the sales team all the resources they need to go out and close deals – whether that's information for them (about the product and the benefits to customers, based on our research) or materials for them to give to prospects (such as explainer videos and digital brochures / sales decks).

Sales might ask for something – "Hey, I need a PDF which includes our prices and information to be able to email to clients" – in which case marketing should step up and provide it.

Marketing might suggest a resource – "Would a video walking through the product be helpful?".

Wherever the initiative starts, the key to sales enablement is harmony.

There's often friction between the teams and that just does damage.

I've been in Sales and Marketing teams where sales has asked for something... but design has come back with something completely different and everyone gets frustrated.

I've also had instances where marketing has spent time on making resources the way sales requested... despite not really understanding why and thinking there's a better way.

Communication and teamwork are the key for the best sales enablement.

It's not the sole function of marketing, but still an important one, to be the pit crew that supports sales.

Brand Marketing

Think of an advert run by a giant company that didn't really have anything to do with their products.

Nike, Coca Cola, those sorts of companies. Nike adverts are often about sports and achieving – they're not demonstrating the product or speaking about the features and how they make you do better. Coca Cola adverts are often about friendship, enjoyment, sharing. They're not promoting coke for the health benefits, that's for sure.

This is brand marketing. They're putting their efforts into building the name of the brand rather than engaging customers intellectually with the product.

Product Marketing

When you're being sold on the features and benefits, it's not the brand – it's the product itself. If a webpage speaks about how light, slim and fast a laptop is, that's product marketing.

If a sportswear brand talks about their new material which is breathable, dries quickly and doesn't wear out, that's product marketing.

The thing about product marketing is you need to remember to keep it focussed on your audience. You do that in three ways.

First, don't get too techy – don't overwhelm the audience with jargon that you understand that they don't.

Second, put more emphasis on the benefit of a feature than the feature itself.

Third, be really visual and descriptive.

So at the end of the day, rather than saying you've got a state-of-the-art personal music device with 5GB of digital storage in a device that's under a centimetre thick, you tell people they can fit "1,000 songs in your pocket". That was slogan Steve Jobs used to unveil the first iPod.

Go back to your Buyer Personas. How does your extensive investment into customer support for your SaaS product help the customer? It's the fact that they never have to wait on hold to get an answer and they're personally cared for.

Product marketing and brand marketing do sometimes meet – Apple being the perfect example. When Jobs would get up on stage to introduce a new product, he'd talk about the features. But it's backed up with one of the world's biggest and most trusted brands – in fact, the entire launch events were brand exercises.

I'm telling you about these different types of marketing so you can differentiate them.

If you're writing a landing page for a BOFU ad, you're probably going to emphasise product and talk a lot about features.

If sales ask you for a brochure or sales deck, ask them for more questions – should it be product or brand focussed? Where in the sales process do they intend to use it?

CHAPTER 10

EVENT MARKETING

Why go to someone else's networking event... when you can host your own?

Host an event your target audience will want to attend.

This is not about getting everyone to come and listen to a sales pitch – no one will turn up and no one will buy (you often find the same with "webinars" that are really product demos).

It's about bringing people together under your roof, to reinforce your brand; put your product in front of a large number of people; capture lots of hot leads and introduce your product as a leader – not sell it straight away.

When I was at university, the rabbis were the ones who did this best. You see, there were hundreds of Jewish students on campus, most not particularly interested in Judaism – let alone attending services in the first weeks of their university journeys.

The rabbis could have just handed out leaflets and tried to get people to come and sign up for synagogue… but they would be competing with hundreds of activity-based societies, nightclubs and more.

So instead, they opened up for a mixer event. Free, lots of pizza, with no requirement to sit through a lecture on Jewish philosophy or law, attend prayers or commit to Sabbath. In fact, there wasn't any lecture – let alone a required one. It was just come, enjoy the food, meet some people.

So everyone came. And entered the pipeline.

At the event, the rabbis could engage with new students directly – after all, we were in their houses – and they could show that they're hospitable people, with open doors for everyone.

They had posters and flyers promoting upcoming events, which people read whilst they waited for food or chatted with friends.

They established relationships and made sure everyone knew where they were – and that's what your event marketing should aim to do.

For students on campus in freshers' week, it's free food and meeting people.

What is it that your audience is interested in?

Perhaps it's a conference, filled with speakers from across their industry and opportunities to meet new colleagues.

Perhaps it's a getaway, to leave behind their stresses.

Look back at your Buyer Personas and ask yourself – what will get 1,000 of these people in a room.

From there, the journey is simple – you market the event. It may need its own offshoot brand. It definitely needs a name.

I recommend charging for most events, because that way you'll get serious players only – but that means you're going to need to market it well.

Your focus in planning the event needs to be 80% how are we going to throw the best party ever (or conference or whatever) and 20% how are we going to monetise this, ensure that we turn attendees into customers.

CHAPTER 11

WRITE A BOOK

I'm going to let you in on a secret here. But keep it between us, ok?

Write a book! If you want to be viewed as speaking from authority, a book puts with your name on it you a level above everyone else with just a blog online.

If you've already got an online blog, you're winning. Because all that content you created over the months and years... you're just going to recycle into your book.

Writing a book is hard only in that it requires the willpower to sit and write. This isn't the first book I've started, you know... but this time, I publicly shared a deadline before I even began writing, so that I would have to finish. Previously, I kept it secret.

That's my motivator. Find yours. If you've got a whole team, use them – assign each person a single topic to write a chapter on by the end of the week. Boom, you have your book.

If you're a caterer for events (or a venue providing in-house catering), publish a recipe book. Fill it with scrumptious pictures, emotive descriptions and great recipes your audience will want to try at home. That's far better than any facebook ad or event exhibition you could promote yourself in!

This isn't about making money off book sales (although it should look like it). The book is a means to an end – reinforcing your brand and validating your authority. Then promote the hell out of it as if you're trying to make money off it – whilst also handing out free copies to prospective clients, partners and other big names.

CHAPTER 12

HOST A DINNER PARTY

There's only so much "adding value" you can do by publishing blogs, books and podcasts for your audience. There's a limit to how much we can consume, a limit to how much we care. These days, your audience is flooded.

Hosting a dinner party (or drinks) may just solve this problem.

The idea is simple: invite around four prospects, with their spouses, to dinner one evening. Pick four people who you think will get on and have a good time together, but who will also benefit in a business sense from knowing one another.

The invitation isn't the same as inviting to a webinar or social event. Your tone-of-voice should change to imply this is social, out of work.

"By the way, next Tuesday my husband and I are hosting dinner. We'd love you to join. James, CEO at Corporate Ltd and Mary, CTO at Company PLC are coming with their spouses. I think you'd really get on with them."

This is such a breath of fresh air – because professionals don't often get invitations like these. It's not a sales dinner – being treated to hospitality for work, but actually costing them a night away from family – but a real, social evening.

There are other good contacts for them there – whether on a personal or professional level (or both), you're promising them valuable introductions.

At the end of the night – if your cooking is up to scratch and you've bought enough wine – they'll think of you as a great guy/girl, who they enjoy being with... a real human being, rather than just another businessperson just interested in making a sale.

You can't fake this – you've got to put effort into the evening, pick a good group of people and not bring up work. They'll talk about business anyway – we all do – and they all know what you do. So maybe the occasional quip, if that's your style, but nothing that turns the evening from "fun" to "work" and nothing that makes them feel awkward.

You can't ask for the sale on the night. If they bring it up, you have to look them in the eye and say, "I'm glad you're interested and can't wait to work with you... but let's talk tomorrow, tonight is pleasure, not business".

The timing of your follow up also has to be carefully considered – I would avoid doing it too fast. Firstly, they'll probably message or email to thank you the next day. They might bring it up then with a question or be ready to sign, in which case you're welcome to go ahead.

If they don't mention business in their thank you message, I wouldn't want to give the impression you're now bringing it up so they feel obligated because of dinner. Give it a couple of days.

Some people will disagree with me here and you'll have individual experiences that prove me wrong. Sometimes, you'll have a wonderful dinner, they'll be all smiles, you'll wait 48 hours... and they'll say "sorry, we're not going ahead".

Hey, that's life. You win some, you lose some. Don't be a sore loser.

CHAPTER 13

SEARCH ADVERTISING

N.B.: When I talk about Search Advertising, I'm basing it solely on Google. Google not only dominates the search market, but all the other search engines are simply doing what they can to imitate Google.

It's beautifully simple.

When you make a search on Google, the first few results are usually adverts.

If you didn't know that, go try it out.

Whilst we're pulling our hair out trying to rank organically, there's a fast-track pass to the top of the queue. Paying to show up.

With Google, you can advertise based on "search terms". You tell Google what searches you want your advert to appear for. You choose between:

Exact Match – your ad appears only when the search term is exactly what you've written

Phrase Match – your ad appears when the word or complete phrase you've written appears, unbroken in the search (but it may have other words before or after the term)

Broad Match – your ad appears when your word or phrase is contained or partially contained within the search term.

Depending on how much you're spending, you may choose to learn to do this yourself or bring in a specialist.

It's not hard to DIY – I've done so – but bringing in a performance marketer is worth it to level up your Search Advertising game.

The way it works is you "bid" for your ad to appear – like in an auction, but a 24/7 digital auction where there are other factors.

You can choose to run campaigns based on clicks (CPC, you don't pay if you're not clicked) or impressions (CPM, you pay for your ad to be shown 1,000 times). There are some other options, but usually that's where you'll want to start with Search Advertising.

Here's the thing though. It's simple, but not that simple…

The story goes that in May 2002, Larry Page was typing searches into Google – just messing around with his product. He noticed that there was a big problem with the ads – some of them were totally irrelevant. Searchers were being subject to ads in which they wouldn't be interested, which would ruin their experience. So Larry Page – CEO and Founder of Google – printed off the pages he was on, stuck them up on the wall in the office kitchen and wrote, "these ads suck" over the top.

An engineer picked the note up, gathered some colleagues and over the weekend came up with and coded a solution – an algorithm to calculate ad relevancy.

From then on, where your ad would appear for the terms you requested (if at all) depended on two things. Your bid in the auction and the relevancy of your ad to the search.

The relevancy has since morphed into a wider evaluation – quality. Your quality score includes a number of factors, beginning with the relevancy but also including loading speed, mobile accessibility and more.

To be successful with Google Ads, you can't just throw money at them… you've got to write good ads, be relevant to the search terms and have good landing pages.

I'm not going to get technical into how to do that, how to price your campaigns… there are plenty of articles, YouTube videos and books written by experts on the details. There are also official Google courses you can do.

Instead, let's talk about how Google Ads can be relevant to your business and where they fit in your marketing strategy.

Your Brand Name

In general, you don't need to run ads for when people search for your own brand name.

I never ran ads against the search term MAGNIV Photomagnets because we'd show up at the top organically, 100% of the time, as well as appearing in the Google Maps information panel on the right (by the way – make sure you've set that up, by going to business.google.com).

However, if your competitors are running ads against your name, it might be worth it. This is very common in the startup industry. Luckily, if you're also running an ad on your own name, your relevancy will be much higher than the competitor, so you won't need to bid too much to show up first.

Of course, there's a limit to how many people are searching for your brand name.

Inquiries for your product

THIS is where the obvious gains lie. Someone isn't searching for your brand – they don't know who you are, yet – but they are actively looking for your product.

It's like they're walking down the high street saying, "anyone know where I can get a pizza near here?" You want to be jumping up and down in your front entrance shouting "here, here, we make awesome pizza, it's tasty, it's fast, we have great toppings, it's the best price, everyone loves our pizza, come here" with a big neon arrow and neon pizza on the roof pointing in.

Of course, there's a limit to how many people are searching for your product – so once again, we need to go wider.

Inquiries for your solution to their problem

So they're not looking for pizza, but they are thinking, "I'm hungry, are there any restaurants around?"

Suddenly you're competing with a lot more people, but you want to be out spreading the smell of your pizza, letting them see the cheese stretch… so then they want pizza and come to you.

Of course, there's a limit to how many people are searching for your solution. They might not have considered it yet. And so we cast the net wider.

Inquiries for a different solution to the same problem you solve

Melissa wasn't thinking of going out to eat. The thought never crossed her mind. She was just searching for, "quick recipes to make for dinner".

But then your ad pops up and plants the idea of pizza in her mind. Not only that, because she's searched for "quick", you're going to emphasise how easy it is to order from you. How stress-free the process is and how fast your pizza will arrive – because clearly, she just can't be bothered for complicated cooking (a sentiment we can all relate to at times). So you're going to solve her problem... but not in the way she imagined.

This is a far wider approach to search advertising – many people will scroll straight past your ad to find what they're actually looking for. It's tough. But if you think creatively and word your ads carefully, there's a lot of potential here.

A word of warning – if you're experimenting with Google Ads yourself, make sure to set daily spend limits and check in daily at the beginning.

The last thing you want is to set up a campaign, come back in 14 days and find you've lost thousands of pounds because your ad is being triggered by a search term that's not relevant.

Now, if you think Google Ads are for you, go and watch a few YouTube videos on how to set up campaigns, how to use negative keywords, how to know how much to bid... and everything else you need to learn. Read some blogs, maybe do the Google course and then just start your first campaigns with small amounts of money. You'll pick it up fairly easily.

CHAPTER 14

START A PRIVATE MAIL LIST

If Content Marketing and Email Marketing had a baby, it would be this.

This is not a newsletter that spams all your customers and never gets opened. Start building an email list that your target audience will want to read – it doesn't have to promote you. Write a short email each week (no more than 400 words, no HTML designs, just a regular email) about a topic relevant to your audience.

For example, I could write about trends in marketing – marketers would sign up to receive a weekly email with a clever new idea, a tool they might want to use, a trend they could get on board with, some advice on a pressing issue... They'd open the email each week because they know the email isn't trying to sell – rather they'll be able to absorb something new in sixty seconds.

If you design, model and fit kitchens in the B2C space, for example, you could send an email each week with a quick and easy but healthy recipe, that would suit any family or professional. Or a tip on how to improve one cooking skill – maybe it's baking better cakes or a hack for chopping vegetables.

If you started a newsletter showcasing your work and trying to sell kitchens, your customers would unsubscribe (they've already hired you and have their kitchen) and no one else would sign up (who voluntarily signs up for ads?).

But your weekly email with a recipe or tip should become something every busy professional and every stay-at-home-parent wants to sign up to – even if they're not looking for a new kitchen – and then tells their friends about. "It's so great, I try their recipes every week and they turn out great".

You start to slip your business in later on. From the beginning, you've got it in your email signature and maybe a small PS paragraph underneath. Then you might move it up – you give the recipe and follow it with "New Kitchen Design of the Week", showcasing one piece of your work.

No outright call-to-action with added urgency and a fancy button ("Click here to book yours before we run out"). But maybe a "send me an email if you want to chat about kitchen renovations ☺".

The point is, this isn't an advert. It isn't another newsletter. It's a personal email that people should look forward to receiving. It should make them feel like they know you quite personally and are privileged to have you share with them.

They should grow fond of you and trust your expertise so that, eventually, either they'll come to you or you'll ask them to buy and they'll say yes.

This approach requires patience but it's low cost and easy to deliver.

CHAPTER 15

CARE FOR YOUR CUSTOMERS

User retention is as important as user acquisition; a part of marketing is creating loyalty to your business.

Ultimately, however good your product is, someone else will also be offering it. That's life.

They may beat you on price. That's life.

How are you going to keep your customers if someone replicates the results you offer and undercuts you?

By making them LOVE you.

How do you do that?

By caring about them as much as you care about making money.

Don't get me wrong – making money is important in business. You have to think about the money. I'm not one of those people who pretend it's all about passion or love. It's about money, at least to some extent.

But if you don't care about your customers, the money won't come. If you do care about your customers, the money will follow.

This works on so many levels, so let's go one at a time.

Firstly, no matter how badly you screw up, if you care about your customers – really care and show them you care – they'll support you and you can bounce back.

Things go wrong – that's life. We're all humans and humans make mistakes. We can't be switched on 24/7. So if your servers go down and it takes a while to fix... that's normal. If you miss a product out of a customer's delivery... that can happen. If you have a car accident on the way to an event and arrive late... that's life.

All of these things have happened to my teams. I could go on.

Staff sickness. Double bookings. Equipment malfunctions. Stock shortages. Family emergencies.

No matter how many contingencies you put in place (which, by the way, is also a part of caring for your customers, because contingencies cost money), things still go wrong.

Trust me – I'm a cautious guy. I plan backup after backup.

But when your lead photographer wakes up on the morning of a wedding in the peak of the summer wedding season with a major allergic reaction… you've got to deal with it. And at that point, you've got to care for two things above all others – your customers and your team. Money takes a backseat.

It's a true story, Sunday lunchtime, I'm on the beach in Spain and get a call from the photographer who says, "I'm going to shower and see how it is". I then get a WhatsApp photo and (as my EMT brain kicks in) immediately say, "there's no way you're going to the event, go to hospital now".

So I dust off the sand, go home and proceed to call every single photographer I know and many I don't know, to try and find someone to cover.

I'm calling people who are going to cost me 5-6 times our photography budget – because at that point, I just had to think about the client's wedding. I was fully aware that hiring one of these photographers would turn the event from a fairly profitable sale into a major loss.

Long story short, no one was available. It was a very popular date and every photographer was booked out. Luckily, my original photographer was feeling a lot better by the afternoon and made it out and pushed through, so we still delivered.

Anyway – back to the point.

You will screw up.

Sometimes it will be out of your control – like my wedding photographer story.

Sometimes it will be within your control and completely your fault (especially as you grow and delegate to staff).

You've got to focus on caring about the people and worry about the lost profits later.

If you're human with your customers, showing you care, they'll be human and tolerant with you.

So put all the effort in to getting it right and to fixing the problems. Put the effort in to delivering 100%, 100% of the time. Don't cut any corners – ever. Check in with your customers. Personalise their experience. Answer their messages quickly. Be flexible with them. Care about them.

So that when you screw up, you've got credit.

It's true that some companies don't care about their customers. In my opinion, Facebook doesn't care about its customers. As a both an advertiser and a user, my experiences with Facebook (the business group, including Instagram, WhatsApp etc) have been terrible.

They've never called me to offer to help optimise my ad campaigns. I've never been able to speak to a human about antisemitic posts that I've reported. I've had a business account deactivated without explanation and been unable to speak to someone to find out the issue (it eventually came back - seemingly an algorithm problem on their side).

Facebook gets away with it, because they've got a monopoly.

But even Google cares about its customers more. In fact, they care about the people A LOT. I've already shown you how they prioritise users over advertisers to give the best experience.

But Google – a huge, global business which has a monopoly on Search and is a main player in many other areas – gives more attention and care to their customers than Facebook.

I've had problems with my business listings on Google Maps – a free service – and I've called up to speak to someone who helped me fix it. I've had emails and calls from experts offering to help with my ads.

Microsoft is the same – better even. When I have a problem or I can't work out how to do something with my accounts, I email Andrew directly and he helps me out. If I don't let him know that the problem is solved after he gives me instructions, he calls or emails me back to check in.

Who is Andrew? Andrew works for Microsoft Customer Support. My emails go straight to him. His working hours are Sunday-Thursday, 9am-6pm EST. He went to the same University as me, but I think that was just a coincidence. He's a human fighting my corner.

If you've ever been into the Apple store for support, you've probably also had great experiences just like I have.

So if Google can give me a call back, even though I've been calling them about free products and from an account on which we spent very little on ad spend... If Apple can take the time to show people how to use their phones 1-1... If Microsoft can direct my emails to a dedicated customer support person who calls me to check in...

You too can care about your customers. There's simply no excuse not too. If you're too small to have a team, you call the customers yourself. I hope that's clear.

At the end of the day, caring for your customers will make you more money.

Many sales gurus will tell you "it's not about convincing people to buy a random product, you've got to solve a problem the customer is having".

Whether or not those gurus are right, if you care about your customers, your "problem-solving" pitch will be genuine and true. And as a result, you will sell more.

Everyone can see through a fake problem-solving pitch.

Think about the things people say when complaining about the government (whichever party, wherever in the world).

"The politicians don't care about us... it's all about money and power"

"They don't get the lives of ordinary people"

"They're out of touch"

"They're all the same"

But when people like a party and when the government changes hands, there's usually a trend of feeling empowered and cared for.

We like to feel important. We don't want to be just another number.

When I was an EMT, this was something we had to remember. I saw lots of people in the same situations – often to me they were boring, sometimes also a bit gross. A paralytic, drunk teenager, covered in vomit. An old person who is feeling weak and has fallen over. Not every call was a major trauma and exciting for me.

Yet although from our side, we were just looking at another standard case, from the patients' side and from the perspective of their families, this wasn't something that happens to them every day – let alone 10 times a shift, 5 days a week.

To them it was scary. It was an emergency. They needed to see us relate to them and treat each person as if they're our only call of the month and the number 1 priority.

They needed us to look them in the eye, hold their hand, say their name and the words "you're going to be okay".

I'm not a psychologist or sociologist or anything like that – but I do know that we crave and desire this personal attention.

So when we feel cared for by a business, we stick with them, we come back to them and we recommend them.

Stick with Them

I've been with the same mobile phone provider for a few years now. Okay, that's partly because when I compared prices signing up, they offered the best contract.

But I have had the option multiple times to shop around and see if I can get a better deal elsewhere.

To be honest, it's not always the best coverage. Some other providers have better signal in certain areas. It's enough to tempt some people to leave.

But I haven't even entertained the idea of shopping around, because of the care I've received.

One month, I ran out of data about 24 hours before my allowances reset. I went onto the app to buy extra, but it said it would take 36 hours – not useful.

So I called up customer service. Who said to me, "don't worry, I'll add 5GB on, for free, to carry you over".

I'm not a huge business customer – my contract with them is just for my mobile.

I'm not a longstanding customer – only a couple of years.

I was willing and ready to spend a couple of extra quid for another Gigabyte of data. After all, I had used my allowance up. It happens, occasionally.

There was no need for them to give me the extra bit for free.

But why would I consider looking for a different supplier when I know that I can call customer service and get a helpful response that goes the extra mile?

So I stick with my provider. Because they have actively demonstrated that they care.

Come Back to Them

My business insurance broker is a similar story. I came to them on a recommendation, looking for insurance for my first business.

I knew nothing about the different types of cover, what I needed, how it worked.

I had started by asking for one thing, but ended up adding various more aspects to the cover. Eventually, I asked Sammy, the new business advisor looking after me, if I could come in to meet with her and go through it all.

She said sure, so I came down to their offices. There were a few dozen insurance specialists there working – so this was a big enough business to not need to put much effort into my little account. My cover was so small, their fee from the insurers must have been tiny.

Nonetheless, when I sat down in the meeting room with Sammy, Oliver the Director came to sit in too. The two of them talked me – a first time, inexperienced, 20 year-old entrepreneur with a micro account – through absolutely everything I needed to know. They spent an hour with me answering every question I had. I left their offices feeling like an insurance expert. Ready to become a broker myself, almost.

But more than that, I felt that they had my back.

They already had my business – Sammy probably didn't have to take the meeting. She definitely could've cut it shorter saying, "this is beyond the scope of the insurance… why don't you email me any more questions" and the boss absolutely didn't need to join the entire meeting. He could've stepped in, shaken my hand and that would have made a nice impression on its own.

But they didn't go for the easy options – they invested care into me. They knew that my business was my baby and they showed me that they would be caring for me and my baby like their own.

So when I set up my next business and needed an insurance policy, guess who I went straight to? Of course, the same people.

And when I set up my next business, hopefully very soon, guess who I'll be going to?

Sammy, Oliver, Danny, Jackson and the rest of the team at Heath Crawford, of course.

Promote Them

I've told you about my mobile phone provider and my business insurance broker. I like them, they seem to care about me, so I'm promoting them.

If you leave your customers with an "ok" or "good" feeling, that doesn't mean they're going to go out and sing about you.

Maybe they'll remember you if someone asks about it... but they're not going to get home and straight away leave a tripadvisor review if it was "Yeah, alright, could be worse".

Let's dig into this.

You've probably come across the Net Promoter Score (NPS) before. It's the question, How likely would you be to recommend (business name) to a friend or colleague?

The NPS results are categorised into Detractors (1-6), Neutral (7-8) and Promoters (9-10).

Anyone who rates your business 6 or under is detracting from your rep – there's a problem that needs eliminating there, which is fairly obvious.

Anyone who rates your business 9-10 loves you and loves your product. We don't go around giving 10s all the time – it's something special.

Those people would be willing to put their name next to your product and testify in a court of law that your product is absolutely brilliant.

They tell their friends and families, they write glowing online reviews and you could probably tattoo your logo on their foreheads.

If your customers know you've worked through the night to deliver their urgent product, they're going to love you and tell everyone.

If your customers are overwhelmed with joy seeing the custom product you've made them and the extra steps you've taken to present it beautifully, they're going to love you and tell others.

They're 9s and 10s.

But the 7s and 8s are neutral. You probably thought an 8/10 rating is good, right? Even a 7 seems like a win.

But it's not a win. It's a neutral. You want your customers to be promoters. You want them to go out and rave about you. So from a marketing perspective, it's a loss.

Don't settle for just meeting the customer's basic needs and fulfilling your contract.

Never say, "who cares", "it's fine" or "we've done our bit" when it comes to customer satisfaction.

Go above and beyond the call of duty to make it perfect.

If you screw up, fix it or refund without being asked.

That's how you turn them into a 10.

Don't wait for the customer to notice and complain.

Because even if they don't complain or barely notice, you're leaving a 7 or 8 on the table.

And that's basically leaving money on the table.

As well as caring, you need to find ways to demonstrate to all your clients that you care. Not every client is going to have a crisis you fix and even if they do, they might not even know about it – all the time in events we were solving problems before the clients would notice.

So you need to actively seek out opportunities to demonstrate your care – without faking it.

Save your customers' phone numbers into your phone, so you can answer the phone with their name, rather than wait for them to introduce themselves. If you use a landline system, look into digital solutions that link to your computer to display the caller name.

Send follow up emails and updates to let them know what's happening – if you're trying to sort something out on their behalf, tell them about the calls you've made, the steps you're planning to take and when they can expect to hear from you.

Get personal – I send happy birthday messages to a lot of people I work with. Not just a template Happy Birthday on their Facebook or the automatic button on LinkedIn, but a personal voice note or video.

At MAGNIV, I knew a lot of previous customers' anniversaries, because we had done their weddings. So for a while, I experimented with sending anniversary cards including a photo we had taken at their wedding.

If you're in the B2B space, follow your customers' LinkedIn pages (both personal and business) and keep up with their news. Celebrate their success with them. Share it with others.

If you're in B2C, listen out for problems your customers tell you about that you can help solve. Maybe it's giving them a phone number of someone you recommend, maybe it's helping out with a slightly unrelated problem that you're able to.

It's all about going above and beyond.

If you lead a big team, you need to empower them to care also.

Have you ever met a CEO or senior manager, mentioned a problem you've had from their company and they've sorted it straight away?

You've been trying for ages with customer service, banging your head against a brick wall. You happen to be sitting on a plane next to the CEO of a software company, who notices on your laptop you're using his program and asks what you think about it. You mention the issue, s/he takes your account number, sends a text to someone in the office and within an hour, it's sorted.

I attended a small talk by JSwipe Founder David Yarus, who is also a thought leader in the millennial marketing space. JSwipe is a Jewish dating app that operates on the freemium model.

At the end of the talk, he said if anyone wanted their accounts upgraded to the premium tier, come and give him their email and he'd have it done. He just jotted the emails down on his phone and later passed them onto someone in his team.

That's a classic CEO move. CEOs make things happen. When you get to the leader with decision-making, action-taking power, there's no question.

But not everyone of your customers is going to be able to come to you, the leader – that's why you have a team.

So you need to empower the team to care and take CEO-style actions on behalf of the customer – just like the guy who gave me 5GB of data for free. At another phone company, the call centre staff may not have that sort of power. In many businesses, staff are pigeon-holed and forced to follow flowcharts and systems.

Authorise and empower your team to advocate for the customers. Whether it's throwing in something extra for free or taking drastic action to fix a problem, the result the customer receives should be the same whether they're speaking to you or to the most junior member of staff.

Allow your team to give refunds outside of standard policy, based on what's fair. Allow them to make changes and break the rules, if they think you would do the same.

Consideration from someone with authority is often all that's needed but there's nothing more frustrating than receiving a "no" from someone without authority to say "yes".

So give your team that authority, whenever possible.

Of course, some decisions will need to go up further than a junior team member. But rather than making it a policy that they should say no, make the policy that they should approach the manager in question and present the case on behalf of the customer – elevate the issue until it is considered, rather than shutting it down.

CHAPTER 16

GO FOR ROUND 2

Mostly, I've been talking about acquiring new users/customers. That said, your existing client base are not precluded from buying again... but it's not an automatic given. You've got to remind them who you are and encourage them to come back. Let me explain.

Your existing audience of previous customers is a great target. They've already chosen you – they've already taken the big risk, so they must have liked you.

I'm going to take it for granted that you've treated them very well, delivered 100% and left them very happy.

So you don't need to convince them that you're reliable and trustworthy. You don't need to prove your expertise. You've got history to back you up – proper evidence.

These are the perfect people for you to target in the quest to generate revenue.

You've even got all their data so you can contact them, whether by phone, text, email or post. You can use their name. You can personalise your messages.

But.

(Of course, there had to be a big but – it was getting too good to be true).

Many businesses overdo this. They subscribe all their previous customers to their newsletter that never gets opened.

And then starts to clog up the inbox.

And becomes really, really annoying.

So you lose your privileged status as a trusted, preferred business...

And go to the bottom of the pile.

"OMG, I used them once and they've been sending me non-stop marketing stuff. It's like, at least 10 emails a week and a probably a text too. Like, leave me alone, I'll come back to you if I want to!"

So we're going to need to prevent that. Here's what you need to look for.

Justification

If your message, call or email has a specific and understandable justification, it doesn't become a nuisance – by contrast, it's helpful.

"Hi Alex, it's nearly 6 months since I last tuned your piano, which should be done twice a year. I remember you work mornings, so should we try book in a time for me to come one afternoon next week?"

That's a justified message – you're making sure Alex remembers to get her piano tuned and you've even made sure to show you remember what times are convenient.

If someone comes to you and purchases a birthday present, you should be making a note to follow up with them a year later (or so) before the next birthday.

If that birthday present was for their partner and you know it, you might also want to follow up before Valentines' Day – that's perfectly justified.

But the more justification the better. So if you can say, "I remember you bought your husband cufflinks for his birthday – you may be interested to know we now offer monogramed shirts and I can have a nice one made, boxed and delivered in time for Valentines'"… you're winning.

Don't try to find tenuous connections everywhere – just use the ones that are actually relevant.

Personalisation

The examples I've already given include personalisation, but I want to mention it separately.

Your follow up with customers should be personal – it is you, checking in with a person you care about – not a machine sending a message to a potential repeat buyer.

This isn't to say don't use automation – by contrast, I think automation is great. But automation has to be used in moderation. And done really, really well.

Because we've all received "personalised" emails that obviously came from a machine, so we're all super-tuned-in to the possibility.

So as much as you have the possibility to be personal, do.

What should I be sending?

That depends on you and your business, but here are some ideas.

Birthdays.

LinkedIn, Facebook… it's so easy to find out people's birthdays and add them to your database.

But don't just send a two-word "happy birthday".

Send a money off voucher, a free gift or something physical. You can even automate the posting out of an actual birthday card, if you've delivered goods before.

Their special news.

Stay connected on social media with your customers (LI, IG, FB, whatever works). Someone get engaged? Did their kid graduate from university? Be in touch with them! You don't need to use it to sell (don't be sleazy) but it will remind them who you are.

Relevant holidays.

I gave the example of Valentines', but there are plenty of other occasions throughout the year to take advantage of.

Periodic follow-ups.

Think about how often someone might re-buy your product. Just like my piano tuner example – it's pretty legit to follow up after 6 months. The same could go for a gardener, getting back in touch at the start of the season.

Connect on Social Media

Being connected with your customers on social media means you're in their field of vision – it's the digital equivalent of them walking past your bakery on their way to work every day. Naturally, they're bound to pop-in and get a coffee and pastry every so often.

Just like you wouldn't stand outside the bakery waving your arms and shouting at them to come in (it's enough that they smell the fresh fragrances of baked goods and see the window displays), you don't need to be posting sales posts all day on social media – but we'll speak about that later on.

Connect with your customers on social media, just so that they remember your name and what you do. Depending on the type of business you run, that may mean LinkedIn or Facebook from a personal account, it may mean following them on Instagram and regularly commenting on their posts. The key is remembering to connect each time you start a relationship with a new client.

Automating Follow Ups

A couple of pages earlier, I was telling you to follow up personally and not rely on automations. That's the best, but automation in moderation is also a really valuable tool because it does the work for you, so let's talk about that.

Tools like MailChimp allow you to build lists of contacts with loads of data. You can import from your CRM, you can add contacts manually, but the key is it's not just pasting a list off email addresses into the BCC line of your regular email client.

These tools use fields that you pre-set to fill information into the email messages.

The obvious place to start is making sure each contact has their first and last names in the correct field, spelled correctly and with the right capitalisation. If you're taking the information customers submit in forms and automatically adding it, check it manually – customers will sometimes just put their initials in the "name" field and then it's really obvious when you've automated an email.

Then you can segment your lists with different traits that apply to your customers. I can't tell you how to divide up your audience – it may be by demographic, by the product they've bought or some other data you have captured.

Instead of sending the same automated emails to your entire list, send it to the right segments.

Perhaps you've tagged your contacts by gender, ahead of Fathers' Day, instead of sending one email to your whole list, you could send an email to the men on your list promoting gifts for their fathers and a separate email to the women on your list with special offers for buying multiple gifts – for husbands and fathers (and of course the reverse ahead of Mothers' Day).

Similarly, if you have titles, you could send an email to women on your list with the title Mrs. different from the email you send to the rest of the women on your list.

It's not a perfect science – sometimes, people will be missing a tag and won't receive an email relevant to them. Notwithstanding, it's a great way to keep your automated emails relevant to the audience.

So as we're being careful and not sending out too many automated emails to existing customers, what can you send out?

Add-ons and upgrades – for customers who bought the black leather briefcase, perhaps they'd like the matching watch and wallet?

Your news – you're allowed to be proud, whether you've completed a fundraising round or you're dropping a new product.

General news relevant to you – most businesses' emails explaining how they adjusted to coronavirus weren't relevant, but a restaurant could email previous customers if they're offering delivery for the very first time, for example.

CHAPTER 17

CREATE A CUSTOMER FORUM

Most of the work has been done for you here by Mark Zuckerberg. I'm talking about creating a Facebook group for your customers/users. Or a WhatsApp group. Or a Slack channel. Whatever.

The best bit? This will free up more time for you!

I got this idea from the team at BoothBook, a specialised CRM used by one of my businesses. They have a Facebook group in which all their customers are together. I now feel like I "know" many of their other customers (i.e. my competitors...) though we've never met. We help each other out. We answer questions. We occasionally complain, but usually we rave and sometimes suggest new features.

Okay, so their product is Software as a Service (SaaS) and the group is largely used for us to answer each other's questions. But by giving us a 24-hour access to informal support as well as the actual company's support team, BoothBook made us all a lot happier. They also get to hear OUR words in speaking about the platform – which they can then use to promote to new customers (more on this later).

Earlier on, I spoke about Buyer Personas, which can be a bit of a guessing game at times. But a customer forum is the perfect way for you to put your existing audience in one (virtual) space and observe what they do. They like your product for reasons you never imagined.

By creating a customer forum, you can create a feeling of belonging with your customers – making them an in-group. They'll feel bonded together and fond of the people they talk with. They won't just be talking about your product – it will be a group of like-minded people who talk about problems they share, ranging from childcare to dealing with GDPR.

Remember what I said in the last chapter about making your customers LOVE your business, so they're loyal to you, even when Sleazy Sam turns up with a cheaper offer for the same results?

I LOVE BoothBook and their forum is part of that. No, I don't feel like the other users are like my family. I'm not into those clichés. But I do feel like there is a strong digital community of businesspeople like me brought together by our common denominator – use of this product. And I do know that I'll get answers to my questions quickly – even when customer services aren't available. And I do know that I can suggest new development ideas and be listened to. All through a Facebook group.

I don't recommend building a forum on your own custom platform, for a few reasons.

Firstly, you'll never be able to compete with Facebook/ WhatsApp/ Slack on their UX. For chatting online, making posts and receiving answers, they dominate. It's their specialty. They've got teams of developers testing things, fixing bugs and speeding up the interface. You're not Facebook. Don't pretend you can compete with them.

Secondly, more platforms are just a pain. Use what your audience are already using – don't give them another platform to keep up with. It's annoying having to go between lots of different apps. Convenience is key and using existing platforms is convenient.

CHAPTER 18

ACTIVATE YOUR TEAM

The Founder/CEO is also often promoter-in-chief. You know the business inside-out and although you've got a marketing and sales department whose job is promoting the business... it's your passion, your baby, your interest, so you promote it all the time too.

Just like the CEO is promoting the business non-stop, despite it being someone else's job... why not activate the ENTIRE team to become ambassadors?

There are two things you need to achieve here. The first is making sure your team has what they need to promote you. First and foremost – knowledge. They need to know the products and the pricing; they need to know the key sales and marketing messages; they need to understand the positioning of the business. In other words, they need to know about all the foundational brand work we did earlier as well as any new or temporary offers your company has.

So make it part of your company onboarding – don't just show them where the fire exits are, open their email account and teach them how to submit a PO, but actually spend time explaining what the business does and going through your BrandBook.

If you're already an established business with many employees, bring them all in for an afternoon training day. Get pizza and no one will complain.

Then send round the BrandBook and other documents, so everyone has a copy. Save it in your intranet or SharePoint. Maybe even have a few copies professionally printed to have around the office.

The other thing you need to achieve is make your team want to promote you. This means they need to love your product, so they promote it without any incentive. It means they need to see the business's success as their success, so they're motivated to go above and beyond. It means they need to be proud and happy in their workplace.

I have a friend who used to work on the reception desk at Claridge's, a well-known hotel in London. She explained that each new employee gets to stay for a night as a guest in the hotel with a friend or family member (including dinner, cocktails and breakfast).

Most hotel receptionists would never ordinarily be able to afford a stay in such a hotel – by contrast, all they see is wealthy guests (often rude) coming in and out, not appreciating the work they put in. They don't naturally share the vision that the Hotel Management and Directorate have, of building a world class institution. All they see is they're required to look perfect and pamper to the demands of people who wouldn't give them a second glance.

But by giving the employees a taste of the experience they're there to deliver, Claridge's let them in on that vision. Having understood it from the other side, the hotel staff can then provide the service London's finest hotels are renowned for.

How can you get your team in on your vision? How can you make them care not just because it's their job?

If a customer walked in and asked a question which you didn't know the answer to, as a CEO/Director/Founder you wouldn't hold your hands up and say, "I dunno, not my area". You'd help them find the right person – even though it's not really your job – and make sure they're looked after. You want your employees to do the same. Trish, the new trainee in Finance, isn't paid to care when she notices a customer struggling as she leaves the office for lunch. But if Trish cares not just about her own job, but for the whole organisation, she'll go out of her way to help that customer for a couple of minutes or call over the right colleague.

I won't lie – making employees care can be really hard. But you can begin to activate your team as promoters in a few, short and easy steps.

Activate your entire team as promoters in a few short, easy steps

One: Send round a key messages document, so everyone is on the same page of how to pitch your product

Two: Share news surrounding your business, so your team feel like they have a stake in your success

Three: Ask your team to go out and promote you.

- Get them to share your updates on LinkedIn.

- Let them know they're able to give discounts to their friends and family (who will go on to spread the word).

- Coach them on how to write LinkedIn posts and other shares, because they might not have a clue.

Four: Get everyone involved with marketing campaigns and explain why their help is valuable.

Why should Jake from HR care about taking 5 minutes out from his busy day to be on Instagram Live with you?

Why should Katie the Developer spend her time being interviewed for you to write a blog? She's got her own job – you do yours!

You don't need to give a lecture on Content Marketing strategy, but it's easy enough to explain, "as the developer, you know the platform better than anyone. We know our bigger customers care about the tech side and read about the specific features in detail before they buy, because they want to see that we'll be able to meet their demands. Featuring your input is the best way for us to satisfy their needs and presenting it as a 'behind-the-scenes' blog rather than a salesy specs page will engage the reader more, personalise the connection and give it authority. We'll flesh out the writing, but we can't do it without your expertise". Boom – suddenly, it's part of her job.

Five: Let it come from the CEO that marketing is a priority.

If your Head of Marketing/CMO/VP Marketing is struggling to get other departments on board, the CEO needs to publicly throw their weight behind marketing.

So next time you have an office weekly or quarterly, the CEO needs to devote an entire presentation to how you're all shifting to a marketing focus and how it's everyone's responsibility. Because everyone thinks they're the most important people in the business and everyone thinks marketing is the least important department in the business.

Six: Make sure they understand your success benefits them.

More revenue for the business means more team incentives and rewards; better working conditions; bigger team and new tech to spread the workload.

If they want a nice office, with free breakfast, good coffee and Thursday night afterwork drinks paid for... they need to help make sure you can afford it.

Every person on every team should be a company ambassador – but you can't just expect them to be. You have to give them the tools, resources and encouragement.

CHAPTER 19

MANAGE REVIEWS

Referrals, Social Proof, Word of Mouth... it all comes down to the same principle.

Use your previous clients as a way to validate yourself in the eyes of prospects.

If you're already caring for your customers (see Chapter 12) and you've got them up to 9s and 10s on the NPS scale, they'll be more than happy to recommend and promote you.

But that doesn't mean they actually will.

In fact, unless you ask them to... they might not bother leaving a review. It's time out of their day and not their number one priority. So if you want to take full advantage of reviews, you're going to have to manage them.

Step One has got to be dedicating someone to manage reviews as part of their role and start measuring their KPIs on it.

You could have a set number of reviews captured per week, if your business is established already and can reach out to plenty of past customers.

You could make it a target for going forward – if you have an average of 250 visitors a week, how many reviews do you want them to collect?

Perhaps the person managing reviews activates your entire client-facing team. In a bigger business, such as a large law firm, rather than one administrator emailing all the customers, the person you designate could work with each partner or associate to contact their clients directly.

However it's done, it has to be made clear that for this person, managing reviews is not an extra... it's a core part of their responsibilities. It's one of the metrics they're measured on for performance. It's their job to make sure it gets done – their responsibility and their opportunity to innovate and initiate new ways of collecting reviews.

If you're a smaller business or one-man-band, collecting positive reviews is the easiest – although you might not have as much time, you're likely to get a far higher response rate as you can simply be honest with people – WhatsApp them and say, "I'm really proud of the work I did for you, but as you know I'm still trying to get my name out there… it's tough, because being new, people don't necessarily know if they can trust me. If you're able to spare me 90 seconds to write a review, it will go along way in helping me grow".

In terms of platform, I think the best place to have your reviews is on Google My Business. So make sure your GMB account is set up, if it isn't already.

Following that, if you've got a Facebook Page, that's also a good place to have reviews.

If people are sending you reviews directly to your email or phone number, you can still use them! Copy the full text into a nicely designed template for posting on social media and add them to your website. Make sure to include a bit of info about them, so your customers know the review is real (eg first name, job, city, date of purchase or review, what you provided them, medium of review).

You can always reply to them and ask that they post the review online… say something like this:

"Thank you so much for your kind words. It means a lot to know you're this happy with the ___!

Could I ask a quick favour though? Would you mind just copying and pasting that text into a review on Google?

People trust reviews they see via Google more than if I just post it on our website, because they know it's genuine… And the way you've worded it is just perfect."

Remember to keep a log of all your reviews, including name, date and the full text.

If you're ever looking to write a landing page or brochure copy and want to find a review that mentions a specific aspect of your business, this will make life so much easier.

You might question why this is necessary, thinking that you'll always be able to find your reviews on Facebook and Google.

But be warned - I've had personal experience and heard stories from others about reviews disappearing for various reasons – people deleting their accounts, platforms marking reviews as spam…

All it takes is one Word document or Excel sheet and your reviews are safe forever. Social Proof is so valuable, it's worth investing the time into a bit of copying and pasting.

Your reviews should also guide your marketing. Replicate the language your customers use to describe you, rather than how you think they'd describe you – you'll resonate more clearly with new prospects.

This applies to products also – is there something positive or negative that repeatedly comes up in reviews? Have people mentioned a benefit to them of your product that you hadn't previously considered? Listen carefully, learn from it all and take action.

Get creative with how you share reviews. Maybe it's putting billboards up around your city with them, maybe it's filming your customers and adding the review as a voiceover, maybe it's getting a celebrity to read the reviews out.

If your customers give you gifts and cards – common around Christmas time or after delivering a big project – consider if there's a way you can share a photo of it on your blog or social media.

CHAPTER 20

GET REAL ON SOCIAL

"IS THIS WHAT I WANT TO POST OR WHAT MY AUDIENCE WANTS TO WATCH AND READ?"

We all know someone who continually posts about their business on social media.

They post on their personal profile. They post from their business page. They post in groups.

Every. Post. Tries. To. Sell. It's all buy buy buy, me me me.

They don't give a damn about you and don't realise that in turn, no one wants to see their posts.

(Sorry, rant over).

Social media can be an invaluable tool, but you've got to know how to use it right. I'm not going to get into different approaches to the different platforms, how to maximise growth with "hacks" or any of that. Pick up someone else's book or read one of the million blogs online for that.

The number one thing you've got to do is get real.

When we're scrolling through social media, we're searching for a dopamine hit. Some people get that through funny and entertaining videos, some people get it through politics and news, everyone gets it through human connection.

Give people what they want. Entertain them. Discuss what's important to them. Establish a human connection.

I follow a guy on LinkedIn called Harry Dry. Harry started marketingexamples.com and he shares exactly that – examples of great marketing. It entertains me and educates me. It's something I'm interested in.

But when I see your ad on Instagram, you're not giving me my hit, you're interrupting it. I don't want to see your ad.

Show me a funny video.

Share something I care about.

Talk to ME.

That way, you become a part of my feed, not an interruption to it. You're a welcome guest – you make me smile – not an intruder who I hate.

Of course, keep it relevant and don't force it (there's nothing worse). I don't need to see the Founding Partner at a City law firm dancing to the latest Jason Derulo challenge on Instagram.

Go back to your Buyer Personas (remember them? Chapter 2? I told you not to skip the foundations) and start looking at who they follow and what interests them.

When I was working for a coworking space, marketing to Startups, Freelancers, lots of ex-pats, digital nomads and millennials, I didn't just write on the blog (and similarly, the Social Media people didn't just post) about coworking and why it's great.

I wrote blogs with links to business podcasts and books I recommended. I wrote about International Women's Day, Diabetes and Breast Cancer Awareness. I wrote about mindfulness, positive affirmations and healthy working habits. I wrote about events in the city and Barcelona's culture.

All things my audience were interested in.

Because – once again – no one is interested in hearing you say how great you are.

If you're struggling, ask yourself the following question:

Is this what I want to post or what my audience wants to see?

Use all the foundations

We spent a lot of time working on building a solid brand; we fought with the positioning and messaging; we invested in quality design and photography.

Don't throw all that out of the window now – keep it front and centre as you go forth with social media.

Canva is a simple-to-use design tool for non-designers (like me). Rather than just sticking your photos straight on Instagram stories and using the text options they give you, why not edit in Canva first, to include your own fonts, add your logo and use your exact brand colours?

Social media is one of those areas that you need a balance. Many people fall on one extreme of not posting because they're worried about not being perfect, whilst many other people post low-quality content which doesn't match their brand, buyers or messaging.

Stay true to your business's identity and all the strategic planning we did. Keep your language and design on brand and post with your Buyer Personas in mind.

Answer every message – but not with an autoreply

Unless you're going to spend ages building a proper chatbot (trust me, it takes proper planning), turn off the autoresponder – it doesn't benefit the customer experience.

Having said that, you should still answer every message, personally. Build connections with your audience online by giving them the time of day.

Not only that, reply to them how you would reply to a friend. If someone messages asking, "Hey, what time are you open until today?" your answer should not be, "Dear Jack, Thank you for getting in touch. Our London branch is open until 1900h and our Manchester branch until 1700h. Should you require any further assistance, please do not hesitate to contact us. Yours sincerely,"

It should be, "Hey Jack, we're open until 19:00 in London and 17:00 in Manchester. Want me to book you in?"

Question: So when can I post from my personal Facebook/Instagram page, sharing my business with my friends?

Answer: Occasionally. Let's say, no more than 3 times a year. And there should always be a reason behind it. You've hit a milestone you're proud of? Share it. You've started a new project? Share it – once. You're in the press? Share it.

You've launched a new product – and I'm talking a big thing that's been in the works for months and may disrupt your industry – share it.

That's it.

Stop with the "support small businesses, invite all your friends to like my page".

You can ask your friends to like your page – occasionally – in a post or by sending out invitations... but make it personal? Rather than just blitzing everyone with "Hey, please like my page"... send a personal (or even template) message explaining how it helps you and why you're disrupting their day for a like.

Remember, the average person doesn't necessarily get it.

CHAPTER 21

QUICK NOTES

If your business is just you, stop saying "we". Be honest, use "I". And no, neither the freelancer you occasionally use, nor your mum helping you out, makes it "we". Everyone can see through it.

Stop selling to your friends. It's sleazy and uncomfortable.

Stop using the word "professional". The only people who describe their businesses as "professional" are people who aren't. And Tresemmé. But tresemmé are a whole different story because their entire messaging is a professionals' product for home users.

Worry less about grammar and more about being understood.

Sales and Marketing are really part of the same funnel / pipeline / journey, whatever you want to call it. It's one process – marketing just tends to be at scale whereas sales tends to be 1-1. But integrate and align the two to achieve greater things.

Put less text on your PowerPoints. You don't want to just read off the screen and if the text on the screen is different to what you're saying, people can't focus on both. Rule of thumb – PowerPoint is for visuals (graphs, images, tables) and the "headings" of your presentation, just like you'd use visuals and headings to break down a long, written article.

No one wants to be sold to, but many people love shopping & buying. This is where great marketing has huge potential and where average marketing fails miserably.

If you're no good at presenting, get good at presenting.

You need good ideas. That's what really stands out these days. Be awesome. Artificial Intelligence doesn't come up with good ideas. You need human creativity. And an atmosphere that allows people to come up with good ideas, share them and action them. Don't create an environment in which people are scared to share their ideas, because they won't even bother letting their minds wander enough to have a light bulb moment.

If you send someone a template message and include the word "personal", they'll always know you're lying.

Make Poetry Great Again

If you're at an event and there's a Q&A, asking a good question is a great way to be noticed.

ROI (Return On Investment – what you get out for what you put in) is important. But stop thinking about it in purely financial terms or you'll never build a brand.

Appendix 1

MENTIONS

Here are contact details for some of the businesses I've used and mentioned throughout the book, in case you'd like to contact them.

Heath Crawford are insurance brokers based in Watford, just outside of London. You can call them on 020 8421 7030.

A lot of my brand and design work is done by Kim at +Sunday (Plus Sunday). She's based in Holland, a great friend and you should definitely contact her for all your brand, web and digital design needs. https://plussunday.com

The cover design on this book and the logo of my company MAGNIV were both done by Georgia Blumenthal, a designer based in Manchester, UK. Check out her portfolio at https://georgiablumenthal.myportfolio.com

BoothBook is a CRM and management system designed by photobooth owners for other photobooth owners – but if you're running any kind of events hire business, you should definitely check it out. It's easy to use, the team are great and it made my life running MAGNIV a lot easier. Oh and you can use the code TTCTY for a discount on signing up (new customers only) https://boothbook.com

OneCoWork is a chain of coworking spaces in Barcelona, Spain. I worked for them for one year in marketing and they were my favourite offices ever. They currently have three sites – one sits *on* the water at Marina Port Vell and is simply stunning; one is next to the central Plaça Catalunya square and is a great corporate space whilst the newest is next door to the historic Barcelona cathedral, overlooking the plaza. https://onecowork.com

MAGNIV Photomagnets is my company that takes pictures at events – weddings and corporate – and prints them out, on-site, as magnets for the guests to take home. https://magniv.co.uk or team@magniv.co.uk.

The Kosher Mask Co is the business I set up during coronavirus and sold on a couple of months later. For personalised masks for individuals and bulk branded masks for business, contact team@thekoshermaskco.com.

The cover photo on this book was taken by Georgia Lubert, another great friend and fabulous photographer. https://georgialubertphotography.com

Appendix 2

Talk to Me

Talk to me. Tell me how this book has helped you and your business. Share your own ideas with me. Ask me questions.

My email is dw@drorwayne.com and I do my best to reply to everyone, quickly.

(No, this isn't consent to be added to your mailing list. But nice try).

I'm on LinkedIn and Instagram. So follow & connect with me – that way you can send me a DM, rather than an email, if you prefer.

https://instagram.com/dror.w (@dror.w)

https://linkedin.com/in/drorwayne

Appendix 3

ACUMEN – THE DIGITAL TALK SHOW

What would happen if you took a podcast, but instead of recording just audio, you brought your guests in and filmed in a state-of-the-art studio in Elstree, the world-famous television hub just outside of London?

I'd say you'd end up with something a bit like a talk show.

But rather than broadcasting the talk show on television, if you released it across the web instead... I suppose you could call that a digital talk show.

So that's what I did.

Acumen is my unfiltered space to talk about 3 topics:

- Leadership

- Business

- Marketing

Sometimes I do it alone (sometimes I go on long rants) and other times I bring guests in. In one week of recording I had a CEO, Rabbi, salesman and singer all come down to the studio… there was some real good variety in the content there.

Because I'm covering three separate topics (though some episodes cross over), I'd recommend scrolling through the episodes and picking out the ones most relevant to you.

If you're a business leader, you might be interested in my interview with Rabbi Sands Milun, Managing Director of the charity GIFT – we spoke about building a culture of giving in businesses and the interaction of the corporate and charity worlds.

If you've just started up or recently decided to "go solo" in your profession, taking on yourself the responsibility to find clients, you might enjoy the episode with Simon Leslie, CEO of Ink Global. Hearing about how the team at Ink work non-stop to bring in customers through some of the most challenging times is guaranteed to inspire you.

I'm not going to give any more spoilers away – plus, there's a whole lot more planned – but do check out the show and as always, I'd love your feedback and comments so please send me a message on social media or email me.

www.ingramcontent.com/pod-product-compliance
Lightning Source LLC
Chambersburg PA
CBHW071508220526
45472CB00003B/949